Winner of the 2002 Transcontinental

ROUGE STATE

RODNEY KOENEKE

Winner of the 2002 Transcontinental Poetry Award

ROUGE STATE

RODNEY KOENEKE

PAVEMENT SAW PRESS

OHIO   2003

Editor & Layout : David Baratier
Associate Editor: Sean Karns
Duck Logo: Joe Napora
Cover art: Charlie Ma
Author Photo: Lesley Poirier

Special thanks to Bruce Smallman and Stephen Mainard for their help
with reading for this contest.

A full recognition of the journals where these poems first appeared can
be found at the back of this publication.

Pavement Saw Press
PO Box 6291
Columbus, OH 43206
pavementsaw.org

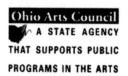

Ohio Arts Council
A STATE AGENCY
THAT SUPPORTS PUBLIC
PROGRAMS IN THE ARTS

Products are available through the publisher or through:
SPD / 1341 Seventh St. / Berkeley, CA 94710 / 510.524.1668

Winner of the 2002 Transcontinental Poetry Award for an outstand-
ing first book-length collection of poetry or prose. We read yearly
from June 1st until August 15th. Send an SASE for information.

CONTENTS

#25 I have seen Grandma's secretion's.

#26 Electric in the rest home, fizzing

#27 Legions of lesions on Janet's hale liver

#28 I saw the show in Tulsa

#29 The harlots of midnight move out

#30 Up what streets are your dependents wandering?

#31 The anxiety of effort, of attempt

#32 Space, then, is time made visible by things

#33 Memo to Britney: watch your back

#34 Gulls hit the breeze to no purpose,

#35 You, a pub quiz Alexander

#36 O.K.—it's Easter Sunday

#37 In this one she's on camera, building a daft chateau

#38 Sprinkle the cavern with pomegranate seeds

#39 How to find safe passage

#40 Shut the fuck up, Grasshopper—

#41 Chief Weemaway at summer camp

#42 Speak of it one time in Portugal, and then

#43 As in the works of Cindy Sherman,

#44 Visigoth Kotex.

#45 First I began an agonizing trip to China,

#46 To execute a prim falcade

#47 Sit, Stella, and fondle my Afro

#48 Is not life more than food

#49 How lovely to shout up to your yacht tonight,

#50 Summer acrostic hotshot,

FOR LESLEY POIRIER,

PAUL TO MY JOHN

they sing for long periods
with a bundle of fire tamarisk in their hands

—Strabo

#1

Impurity's the watch-word here; you get that the minute
you step off the boat. A few hours paddling the lake that forms
the liquid circumference of the conference center
and it's high time to skim from the Captain's indiscretions
more saucy affairs of your own.

While the steamer offers comfort
it poses other, deeper problems: the boiler room
and its touchy valves, the co-pilot sounding the shallows
with his game day leg, the cook of a menacing
and indeterminate mien, whose idea of luxury starts and ends
with gazpacho every night.

But somewhere the jungle offers recompense.
You watch the tendrils pleat a slinky grammar
over the dumber parts of the river
and wonder if they'd bear a human weight—
a swing from those limbs would be delectable,
almost sexual, like the pink and white flora that cruise downstream
with their flushed, brazen orifices unflexed for all the world
to sniff and see. Night smells, the insipid chatter
of baboons, evoke nacreous visions of openings
beyond the frontier: a lush, unspoiled loveliness
around the next muddy crook of the next river over
of a kind no pilgrim your size has ever seen.

And this, too, carries its freight of pleasures
which is also the obverse of a certain boredom:
the rush of not knowing what to praise
meets the roar of the urgent press to mean
not in any straightforward, symbolic way
but just in a general tam-tam of the drums
that bang at night in time to your iffy breath
and unmanning requests to the headman
for an escort past the falls.

A bevy of insects or something to keep loud with,
water and syntax, an enormous ebon slave
is what you might need to make it out here—
a tribe of scribes to ink your winsome hymns.

#2

Caravansaries cavorting invite too hot desires,
florid with houris last seen on the davenport
la-laling in mindless, premenstrual joy.
The clocks here move in cycles, cities thrown up
by the dozen sway
in endless golden smogs.
Our luck rests on a camel lash, on the lap
of the sultan in the absinthe tent
who plays oud nights at the liquor store
and phones home for more cheap bud.

Babak's complaint was heartfelt
but he got his name inlaid too soon in jade
across the wrong alfalfa furze. Odd and red,
like betelnut. Tougher to crack than it is to use.
But your hard line re: jazz on Ramadan
made waves in a whirlpool already slick
just that much worse to ride.

Break out the schnapps when you hit the canal
and we'll pour our Applejacks in cups too small,
crumb-bums of appetites earthier
than the maize we started for. I like you,
like the leaky stars, how the moon disappears like nasturtiums
in my unexpurgated nursery rhymes—
first filched from the slave girl's navel
then nibbled by inky-black doves.

Some weeks later out of Tours, fresh down
from the Ministry of Air
I asked the PM to switch his stance on
the India Bill, and go ahead and sign.
A swift octet of bullets against the motorcade
stilled that. Nor did such action escape the censure
of those others fresh-hushed by our rising esteem
in the hetman's roving eye. Their flapjack provisos
called for prickly codicils of self
to which we would never, ever accede.

Was there a God? And could we negotiate new terms
with creatures so far up above our state?
'Pop' Warner lost a leg in WWII
then joined the ranks of Freemasonry
for waffle breakfasts in the expanded parking lots
of our newer, more intimate malls.

I guess you'd call us happy: sleepy, a little cranky
but on the whole well-fed. Back at the ranch
they're searching folks for wing nuts
and airtight basketballs. The metrics are odd
    but I like the good bread
here where our frou-frou tights make camouflage.

#4

You feel almost bad for the Babylon whores
asked to make it *pro bono* on the temple stairs
half-baked, then half-soaked by the oily intrusions
of rain. This one's my favorite, Johanna. Magnificently bored
right before the money shot, then feigning drowsy interest
at the first fat early drops. Wizard behind a Kansas
of Valvoline, wet mammal in a planetarium
all shark. One moves slowly up the ranks,
another one makes it with trampoline ease.

I guess you'd call this one Dr. Johnson,
immense, but with a certain imagination
not seen much in the bush leagues these days.
Won't do the Asian babes, indifferent
to the proverbial 'green door,' yet nobler somehow
for the camcorder screams, upstaging our favorite
laureates of moan. Queen on the speedway, a spa
of one's own—drugless and useless
but still making the scene, introduced
to hot new friends as *pussyboy*.

#5

Richer than maple but still
    like simple, sweet.
Amped up to the be-bops behind your back
cutting out hearts for double happiness
    in the soylent putting greens.

To feel magnificent in Underoos
    disporting from wooden piers with ampersands
    forgiving eyes for ovoids
reducing the carpool with supersized
    knuckle-dust sandwiches
in deference to the boss's new pince nez.

When business picks up things feel that much more
    only more so, like spring in its sneezier symptoms,
the hay piled high, combustible, fertile and tight
in the teen night scratchy with stars.

Keep quiet by moonlight and squint down
from the parachute stars.
Night thoughts looking as cold as us.
The language we learned was
like opened parasols: small, purplish defenses
against the heliotropic bombs.
Dumbed down to fresh situations
we watch the slow ebb of eternity
and dress up the chirping cicadas
in a high-literary sort of way.

Quarks start their fires indifferent to us, a low gas
makes the terrain here almost visible
at wide, uncertain intervals.
The physicist asks for the boyar's helve—
streaked fletchers stick up stagecoaches
and monopolize Tsarina's pretty lines.

Stand-to's at sunrise: you'll want to brush up
on your corner shop Greek
to make mild new terms with perfection, whose
white flag's that much brighter now than yours.

A half -life in ingenious drag. Deep maps to places
We can't go, marked *oubliette* or *razorblade*
Or a word I thought of driving home, then didn't write down
Then forgot. Some place where even shaving has its meaning, its
lesson
Of *weltschmerz* or absence or something like that
Into which truth might be precipitated like a virgin sacrifice,
A defenestrated Oldsmobile, now rusty and weedy and
home to the mice.

But I came here speaking of something else . . . Tiresias pissing
In the stadium trough, bitch goddess asquat the clogged men's stall
Dick tucked back, squeezed hard between the thighs—
A secret. Socks bulge over calves, over clouds stretched pink
and lycra-tight

Across the rainy gold expanse of sky.
Great fucks for the wheat god; next in the series
But glazed with a new penny shine. Orpheus is jailbait,
Touching goth girls, and down here considered bad, bad news—
The bold ones leer and the nice ones squirm.
A text of conjectures: *echt*, ambiguous
And housing air-starved zeppelins all its own.

This is my Inuit, this my best suit
And this is my vintage Willendorf
Brought up from seas green and mild
As Thermidor. It divides into two, and afterwards three.
Look, there's a woman; there, a tired girl.

Arguably a cicada,
folding its wings into hymns.
Or maybe the scars from where your bumpy homunculus
used to squat—I know a good aloe
for that. Or what about the tubing
in the Professor's bamboo lab, where he made
all those tiny, diamond-shaped marshmallows
we zinged at the senators' heads?

The whole bus is utterly silent.
At the end of this broadcast, I will be donating
the proceeds to a charity that works
with the silent. After that, I've scheduled an extensive cruise
across the bruised Sargasso of white male sexuality.

Don't laugh at me in these droopy puttees.
Like the novel makes society visible to itself,
they point to a time when our orders were
much simpler. Now a little funicular takes you up the hill
to a fashionable retro tiki bar.
Yes, I had just finished making an important executive
                                        decision
but I swear I never touched her: larger process
was hard at work, & Look! you are already reading
to the end of its document.

Mammogram the bildungsroman, induce
dingbat hexameters in the heldentenor's
yeasty Hornitos. Queen Ixnay to the E-bay
goes Braxton-Hicks on mother's bad milk day.
Computer's at last completely stewy—
picked up a bug at the honor bar. Citizen Quiggley
from the Gun and Doll Commission seeks flap
with pointillistic gabardine. Bad weekends for
two straight quarters—look inward and talk
to the polygraph: Have you grokked
Hampton Hawes today?

Hey, they were fisting my peoples
on the Road to Hematosis. In what woods were you,
Goody Hooper? We were mewling lords of power
in the Gallery of World Sculpture,
waving from the piazza
with the rabbi's seltzer bottle. Come, Selma
and scotchguard the rainbow
to the john of the Sunset Room. Give us an 'E'
for unpleasant Effordent. To cry 'uncle'
in a wartime theater, that

Was all our pleasure: to swap knuckles
with a gorgeous case of tartar. Yes,
we were all feeling Amish. Denver, please bring me
my omelet pan and we'll bang at the congressman's gams.
I have seen the gated community, and it looks
a lot like us. Hiss fireworks, steam
the Atlantic—green sleestack, be all that.

Sore and recusant in Memorex,
gradually flooring the hupdie
past Coach Gimpy's three-yard line.
Another stark error in the fan letter genre
will not be conceded to cocopuffs
like us. Chet went down fast
on the tomatillo sauce. I feel crappy and warm
in this snappy suit, but that was my best shark,
Sherlock—now get less close to the brie.

Two men so abreast is never beautiful. Morning
becomes geriatric, whistles past commitment
like the moon on a bad shopping spree. What's a palindrome
for baby pants? For the Emperor's new
Model T? For the replicants
that tug our homeland's pigtails? Pssst!
Check out that nervous disorder
with our blisters on her fingers. Barkeep,
that'll be two lobster bibs. Mi casa
is probably your nightmare—a controlled rite of
protuberance from Cap'n Itchy's panic room.
Staying distinctive in the Department of Beautiful People
is not that complex a process:
just tweeze your kestrels really hard
and blow.

Late for the powwow, then the Two
Towers fall. The sheik don't like our wampum.
Bourgeois hobbits scrapple from the Apple, score
dime bags of pipe weed on Avenues C & D.
The poppy crop looks good this year—our Mordor
grows more porous. Et your shoes, Brute,
come from Thailand. But even if my Yugo
sputters dry, transnational orcs
in Cisalpine retreats will still find tips to swap
on Rivendell, Alamos needing Frigidaires,
Shires to wire from Medicine Falls to Chittagong
with us to turn the turbines
in the glitzy manufacturies of consent.

Who spiked the stockade with Injun skulls?
And why were they invisible before?
The fish half of the mermaid, all protozoa
and foam, lifts tips off the bar with her fish tail—
Garcon, may we have the spare room?
The girl half stuffs her frayed brassiere
with Sarge's dirty euros, here to pick off stern emirs
on Chief Sweetcheek's lush back nine.
High elves of high finance float Concordes
off the Golden Westernesse. Kimo Sabe sunburn,
get real red. Smart money at Fort Malfeasance
has us galumphing up on army camels
in ghost shirts and love beads, naked,
beneath the hooves.

#12

The gates of horn conceal five pounds of lunchmeat.
What dad calls dimestore/gumbo tough
is Miguel, your avenging angel
here to announce an eminent demise.
Ella's crazeology too skanky
for my brisket: cleat dick south paw relay—don't edit
yourself, Divine. An experience of total marine freedom
just bubbled past my sleep debt
and the Lipchitz of *poetry concrete*
stopped hitting me in dreams.

I was working the Mollusk Table
at the ankle tattoo convention, a marriage
of beauty and prudence not seen
since Grandma Clabber's gin team days.
Professa, me so honey—
can't keep the poultry straight
without a bank card. Immediately notify the pee cam
should Elspeth lash the Golden Chersonese.
It's SAFE and FREE sez house expert, St. Gregory
still inky from the 'zine lab
singing *ipse dixit* to a shufflepuck.

#13

I owed my happiness then to rhinoplasty,
a short run of articles called *Sex Secrets of the
Ancient Egyptians* and a kind of crafty pimping
of my mom, teaching latch hook and decoupage
to the embassy brats, who in turn lent good ears to
her litany of soft-serve 'facts,'
like hip-hop came from Romania and AIDS
was a whacked hacker's plot.

Burned out from my own deceptively simple rise
I swapped what I could for lapis beads, stashing lolly
against the President's immanent demise.
Life rose to its spotlight of big moments
but was overall quite dull, leaving weekends free
for power journaling
amidst the hip-hop of the corncrakes
just outside the temple walls. Too little fickle sunshine
to supplement all that heat. Vapor trails of memories
freaked out the best in the end
till you couldn't look up at a silver plane
dropping languidly into the airfield weeds without
feeling like atoms in a cyclotron—bright at first
with promise, then curving into alphabets
containing mostly 'O'.

One feels like nachos, then comes to feel
how much depends on the very small dreams
how far you can go with these minor aches
and, when the evening Ouija finds our stars,
what sense it makes to call "lights out" to the Zodiac
where the cool orbs sweat to be distant
and the dorky ones laugh back at us.

#14

Seaplanes crashing through windowpanes,
Moon passing river in paper cup.
The camels get restless—God whistles
through the night like lewd boys
at the prison wrestling squad.

The Magi know their Atari—
long drives from the bar to vacation bible school
sear in the hotter mercies of the East
that leave one a-melt at landingstrips, a sherbet
too orange for summer afternoons
ready to be licked up into tongues.

#15

Here at the garden's hot marges
events soften into fire ants.
We cock ideas at prairie dogs
to watch them smoke, then squeal

Pythagoreans cross their 't's
with dim narcissus fresh-picked from the clefs
of that vast, inaudible cosmic symphony
the cow thieves once called home.

Zeus lets fly with the lightning rods, his
hot heart flaming like shish-kebabs
off a Deer Park backyard grill. Marshmallows
crisp to swart mothers, I burn—pterodactyl
dactyls sing over me with ease.

#16

Excavate the Mexican game show host
for Persiflage of the Nanosecond. Get him
to trickle hot pink verbs
over somebody small and unimportant.
Tell him to titillate the Sefiroth
canoodling with a hot canzone
fresh from Schenectady, her wilting monstrance poised above
the god of forgotten celebrities. Get someone
to loll in the present
while Time preens on the digicam,
trash-talking the Past as History.
Make someone else catalogue
the archive of winged things
encircling the surf. You, in the air, you indomitable
                    doves,

Come down here and pick at the leavings
of my lunch. So the mind rumbas with obeisance
to the throbbing timbales of materiality. Buy me that famous record
by Mister Mister, which adheres to a crucial personal
memory—chewed gum stuck to the mind's inner fridge.
Bring someone who feels Albigensian these days
as I do, a regular Toussaint L'Overture
of the verdure denoting the popular—the type to
make eyes at Night's disjunctive muse,
then wake up as fresh as a Nike swoosh
awarding impeccable sunsets
to nabobs with spotty culottes.

Erik the Red on Kickpoo juice
meets Kid Hiawatha in angry fever pants.
Hippocampi bleeding through a perfect doctor movie
complete the tall cotton: here there be monsters,
here my glum anemones
caterwauling for Poncho, bootylicious
in spangled robes.

Rayodes squat on Tonto, always—
Lugosi vamps for morphine
On the plattes of Saskatoon.
Madrassas in Pakistan await my demise
vasectomied and playing clinic jazz,
unstable as a mismarked isotope.

A prehensile sense of freedom
protrudes from your garden zendo
where the merest sip of innocence
clears the mind of theory,
controlled burns or erasures
that bloom as peonies.

Everything graceful about yourself
goes into the poem: Today I loom hugely
over the commercial parts of the city,
an oaky copse stout hearts do sometimes wander in,
brazen as mariachis
in a moment of vast inattention
where everything happens together, a glimmer
inconstant as Zeus,
fecunder than succotash.

#18

My monogram on the jitney cab,
my tubular bells in the gloaming
of Angkor Wat. What?! Welcome to winter's museum
of soft 'n' greasy Aztec things. Ipecac lineman
on a bad heart day, squished in the broad magnificence
of my voluminous Aeron chairs. I can double your
chewing pleasure by means of these
low salaams to the possible,
unlodge the patroons of Albany with a
quick call to Ivanka in the Bangkok Room.
Think you've got trouble, Papillon?
Try getting Captain Earache
past the velvet ropes of sunset, try cutting bad carbs
from grandma's bul-go-gee.

My head stopped hurting after drinking, and I worried a lot
about that. *My* anesthesiologist
skronking left coast vocalese
on the ample yet cranky Victrola
I stole from the old mountain home.
When did the world-tree, Yggdrasill,
get so deciduous? When Giuffre got the business
from some third-stream Herr Ludwig von Krupke
out behind Maximus security ward.
                                    Ich wolde ich were
a threstlecock, practicing Hollywood dentistry.
Sergeant, please frag this strabismus. Behind each incisor
lurks a Dunciad. Congealed into hip-hop
and frosted, it'd be a swell cover of you.

#19

Consider the lilies
disappearing world presidents
shiver me flivvers
   on a flanged minidisc

I sleep, but my heart keeps risotto
in a perfect sitcom kitchen
abutting a resolution
   to slalom like Olympians
past the moguls of surplus repression

My sensei, Uncle Virgil
wiser than Kabbalah
distributing free samples
   in the precincts of karmic disorder

Winter, winter comes to mountains.
Snows, snows shut the falls.
Long have I waited
   at the star-studded galas
now my benefits have expired

and I work with eucalyptus
at the local necropolis
rubberizing catafalques
   intaglio'd in polychrome

#20

Moist moment of beginnings
in forests that felt too old.
I thought I should find feelings there,
another sweet Jack to swing lantern light with
down the Third Street railroad tracks.

I thought to find an Eden
to find the same but even more
Julys of several sparklers
a night spent reading God's dumb braille
a hot gush of something over the lips
sunspots rising like honeypots, heavenwards.

Sweethearts of what rodeo? Which ambergris?
In the crenellated head of whose narwhal?
Cocktail trays afloat in swimming pools
tell tales of light and simple fats
that crave the all-devouring, mother-minded sea.

Black waters to which river? What bodacious waves?
Some macho Artaud on a longboard
anxious to ride the last glassy one in
for shore. Whose head? On what ottoman?
Mom looking menopausal
and stitching up sonnets for the boudoir drawers.

Which Volvo? Captain of how much
destiny? I'll take the one with handlebars
that depilates the fuzz from grandma's sneer
makes films as scratchy as Sasquatch
sods lawns in the lure of whose clover?
What whisper? Which horse?

#22

T.T. first spotting New England
then learning the Chumash hymns.
My sofas healed up with felicitous daubings of green

as seen on T.V., but more sweetly, like
herbivores in starter homes
turn *autos-da-fe* into autos by Ford, as earth

cranks out the WonderBread
and tries to look sublime.
I carry my alcohol discreetly

through the airports of a fitful century,
vibratoless as Sinatra
in the close Hoboken gloom.

A picaroon hits a banana peel
and somebody sings about that—
Beauty absconding with Meaning

in Dad's 'Jungle Breeze' bubble top van.
Content met Form
at the antelope dance; Diz fizzes

eternity's seltzer
and the kids of dysfunction swing.
The guys at Irvine Nissan

seek Doors of Revolving Perception—
the moon's a moronic romantic
that's silvered my bathroom too long.

Eternity pricks like a phantom limb.
The NASDAQ continues to drop and rise.
Horus with his featherweight
      comes up a little short;
houses waver gravely—first yours
I think, then mine.

Beneath the domes of the future
lurks the Moloch's planetarium
spackled with rat shit and bumper cars
snapped off from their voltage poles.
Sometimes we follow great phalloi of flame, sometimes
      strafe forks in ice cream
set aside for other tribes.

Tell dad we left the oil biz
And lo, the mottled milch-cows gave more milk.
It's something of a myth in parts of Texas—the way
the oil gurgles under hills, the lubricious way
the stars ungauze themselves, reminiscent of a houri's
underclothes. Light roars down a disused gulch

To join more light. Now we meander
at the fringes of a world situation
that isn't all that familiar: shrimp minstrels
      in a world too small
to piss people off in, denizens of pleasant,
reasonably segregated cities
where views can be passionately exchanged
      across vacant public easements.

Like a pinball machine checking itself
for stuck balls, I wonder how precisely
I'm in touch with my position here,
      a wisenstein with slugs
of the Republic on his breath,
tootling a hautboy
from the sloop of global English
aimed at the *farolito*
that puts little stars on the bay.

#24

To take this body back to its first ocean
To slip into ideas like dinner clothes
   To make expensive cell phone calls
From this complete and not unpleasant
Architecture, that adds a certain structure
   To the horizon of watery lights
Whose points wink into storyboards, or not
Depending on what you have or haven't read.

To bathe in the glow of divers' lamps
Titanics listing on rusty sides,
   Stroked by the ocean's green pressures
Jiggling the stateroom and ballroom doors—
   To see a gone world in upturned chandeliers
Doing their best impression of the stars.

I have seen Grandma's secretions.
I have dressed in Auntie's pantyhose.
I have discussed gender issues with the sager of the amoebae
In backstreets watched by perfumed gendarmes.

I have worked the alphabet at Mother's séances,
Chauffeured the local diva in a succession of teal minivans.
I have wrapped the flag round pre-made Safeway sandwiches
And arranged chaise-longues on the Maharani's private lawn.

I have watched pacific oceans
Disgorge their slimy wares.
I have crammed foolscap with poems
And suffered Euterpe's brisk stings.

I have traced the airplane's lemniscate
Over lands very foreign to mine.
I have called down spooky objects from my airspace
And in turn given boomerangs a veranda on which to land.

I have brunched in strip clubs with soccer moms.
I have gazed upon the Torah behind curtain # 3.
I have dropped to my face during fire drills
And stammered canned prayers to the Indian goddess of flame.

I have dandled the lesser Muses on my knee
I have lost the OED, my better half.
I have sunburned beneath traffic lights
And cooled under moons by the Bros. Lumiere.

I have clasped hands with the former century
And I, too, made my peace with fey Walt.
I have placed ebon dildoes on the coffeetable
For Mary to find out with the plumbs.

I have conjured orchestras with swizzle sticks,
Picked up failed dates in airport bars.
I have danced with singing girls in lean-to yurts,
Blown duodecimal jazz from the vulval conch.

I have collected brown envelopes from P.O. boxes,
Taught square dance at the local Sunday school.
I have built a chocolate ziggurat of after dinner mints
And snacked my way to its dark, funereal bowels.

I have entertained a taste for Nembutal
And find it weaker stimulant than sound Welsh tea.
I have indulged a secret lust for tummy tucks
Then banged up my body like an unclaimed airport bag.

My foyer is dark with pink and womb-like silks.
Beneath this heavy sweater, I can't breathe.
I resolve to make an ending. I politely decline to begin.
Double yet sterile; beginning, I end.

Electric in the rest home, fizzing
across its vestibule
dog-tired, incandescent, octoroon
whose dog-eared god wants Ovaltine
and you implore him to accept
your favorite prophylactic brand, slip that instead
in the pan. The Good irradiates
the Great. Hot grease explodes
from the engine room, glubs out
to finger through corridors
for what you earthlings call "great skin"
on which it can place burns.

And you're left with a sexy cicatrix,
an ovulating platypus, a fencing scar
carved tellingly in the left half of that
petit soufflé, your ham. Charon wants his ball back
and yes, that could be fax static on the line
but it also might be Uncle Mort
you know, from the *other* side,
cracking wise about wooden nickels
and the ineluctable need for last year's hunting caps
if you plan to take the Caddy down to Lethe,
sad doggie bags of grist and bone you are.

Breathe easy without your inhaler
and demand your interdicted smokes
by name—mentholated curlicues
of sulfur, methane, bog gas
rising from your head like laurel wreaths
like dawn steam off Lake Garda
like the last pump of that little solid state machine
which brought you here and used to work
your heart, till you went all soft & watery
distinguished by naught
but these marks: a wen,
a golden bough, a portmanteau.

Legions of lesions on Janet's hale liver
no god, she said, blunt as that.
Time for the little dreams, toucans
& cannonades,
Moon a pierced tongue
In the guttermouth night.

The body removed like a vacuum bag
From that chrome gleam,
       consciousness—
The dead part touches the live part and then
The whole thing, it pivots or turns.

#28

I saw the show in Tulsa
  and it tasted pretty good—
Isis swapping underpants

With the Wizard behind the old-
  time photo booth. Mom slips
into something more porous—

Originary, protozoic, chic.
  I'll trade you two dactyls
for half that calligramme;

Then take all this and you'll have
  all this. If the cabby's duked a twenty
he'll swing you on out to the donkey show

Where thought slips off its jackboots
  and sells you a peep for a song.
If you're into sound spankings or Jell-O

Shots, leave Betty and Sis on
  the pig farm back in Witchita,
the one that Grandpa had, you meant to sell

But sadly tried a little swine instead,
  called the dead back into quiet things,
petit, not *gran* convulsions

On the phone line out the barn.
  It hits in spurts, a spending
teething the last of your bullion

Till you're caught with Anubis, all hot
  in tights and vinyl chaps and
begging for feathers to grab.

Last time I checked, she was empty.
  I changed the plugs
and got rid of Dad's magazines

But the shed burned anyway.
  Here, here's the end of my trinkets.
The Dairy Queen? She slunk off thataway.

The harlots of midnight move out
by the evening star.
Lo, I raised my emblem over Nineveh

    And down came a pleasing rain. . .

Bed down in the drowsy Mithraeum,
wake up a castrato in puce chiffon
      menial to the chief androgyne
who leads the sore members of his tribe
on long walks down the Aventine
      exposing horny emperors
dolled up in natty drag.

The moon unsheathes a little ways,
      an oystery pulp in the night.
  Light abrades light
like the distichs in my wittier dirges
rub ankles with a pensive inner state
      that knows itself shinola
while preferring it to shoes.

The transmogrifications of blue around the stars
suggest the early withdrawal
      of light,
a bricolage of useless things
      arranged like the words in that funny patois
our den mother called *disarray*.

Come, put your head down, Kallisthenes;
inventing that jogging machine
      was hard,
thinking alone on an abstract plain
      where nothing should have moved.

The harlots of midnight move out
by the evening star. Lo, my giant emblem
      over Nineveh I raised

    And down came this pleasing rain.

#30

Up what streets are your dependents wandering?
Do you know where your kidneys are?
Homogalactic, we suck
the same milk—dad's gone
and the bathroom is ours.

You stroll the compound with a kind of
bemused detachment—these were your orders, this
your prize squaw. The sacrificial altars
were doubtless in the last days
overused, clogging with entrails on weekends
enough to drive any corporal to booze.

Tomorrow's a day auspicious
for your transfer. When you're finished
with that, let's dance
to some weird form of reveille,
admire the colors in native flags or,
if you want something more forbidden
I think I can manage that, too.

Eating and sleeping in railroad yards,
fishing for coins from the glacier's
crevasse—is there any chance, people,
we can do better? Attitudes flickered
through the cricketless night;
when we hit the first skull we set down our
picks and stopped the excavation just
long enough to thaw

While English went up like an office block
with some of the cubicles yours
in which to build shelves for this year's
Australopithecus-of-the-Year Award, which carries
no money, but a certain raffish
glamour, having won the last
one and the one
that you won before that.

#31

The anxiety of effort, of attempt
that nudges your soft raft of crepe
and crinoline, so it waterlogs
just in advance of Genius Falls
and you come out all dripping and
feel a voyeur

          on O'Hara's last night—
     or no,
the summer yutz who plowed him down
macho, collegiate and hopelessly blonde
and Frank calls you (last
words) his jock queen.

We spill in the world into genders,
fall out like dirty turpentine
from an upset coffee cup—at first
abductees of the harem
refusing silk pillows and gold-tipped cigarettes
then gradually learning to simper and
sprawl, flipped eagerly over
stuffed ottomans
hoping the emir picks me.

Space, then, is time made visible by things
so that when the empire strikes back
it's at air, and hits the mustachioed subalterns
           of the preceding century
with a force that splinters our bleacher seats
in history's cramped stockade.

Just as the phallus devolves into a crocus
or a tower in which the old woman's grandchildren
might live, so does the stodgy mulatto
at last learn to swivel in the captain's chair
and insists on your presence tonight at dinner
near the bowsprit, towards the wake.

Was it we who sparked the problem,
seeing rainbows in others folks' oil spills?
Or us who deserve credit
for getting the flywheel to purposefully oscillate?
Whose physics hipped the groundlings
to the city's architecture:
ships anchored snugly in the estuaries,
guns poking up at the quays?

Probably April will change us, after years
of gamma rays. The cannonades may be
less terrible; hot couples without much scruple
will tamely saunter the esplanades.
It will be Sunday and people will get boozy
behind the modular barriers surrounding the Civic Center.
We were only making literature:
       Space, then, is time made visible
             by things.
My greatest achievement that summer
was keeping skinny, while the boulevards
were filling up with words.

#33

Memo to Britney: watch your back
especially when the dudes of summer yap
    the beaches get disputatious
and the reef wants your hues for its own.

Here we burn our offal
and here we name names
    of sexy movie stars.
You have trampled every distant land

In your slick-as-olives body suit
    and liked it—
way souciant about the erotic
but ignorant of that grimoire
to change men back from swine.

Look—it's raining princes,
the asps have gone
albino, the muffled screams
    of the girls downstairs

We sealed in legal envelopes
for crumpling at the premiere.
    We sailed for a place
where the babes could bronze. I listened,

Ears waxed, at the masthead—
heard every clump on the bookstore step
    as if it was maybe yours.

#34

Gulls hit the breeze to no purpose,
with a snotty air of menace
hanging above the Victorian pleasure halls
    attitudinizing as ruins
on some significant Greek beach.

Look how the pines learn to bend,
    then brood—
that's an image of you,
of your music, mooning at teens
paired up in parking lots

To the urgent lollapalooza
    of the seals
insisting that sex is more sexy
against the backdrop of the ocean's
            uselessness,

Its monstrous investment
in helpless things—a tree, a boot,
    a Ferris wheel
over which mastiffs can run.

Night opens up her superstore
    and puts out the discount stars
in time for their midnight photo shoot,
a sepia daguerreotype
where here there's a pillar
        here a stern fern

And we all hold our breath
for the blinding flash
that assembles us into gradations
        of white
against the vast and talking blues
formerly known as sky.

You, a pub quiz Alexander
and me, a Nefertiti of the bunco squad—
to take this business lying down?
The gender of information suggests
that suffragettes hide curves
under dirty burkahs. Your answer,
        lathed piano keys
is final
and gets at a certain sense of labor
but not the one our girls were looking for.

Catch me, I'm feral
and short on breath. Behind these tannins
lurks a palate blonde
as any Janissary's,
snatched from the village to serve out his years
as a grunt in the mullah's cortege.

Gender is an empire
run on sesame and tea.
If saltness lose its peanuts,
who oils the sno-cone machine?
Good wine in peevish wineskins
dries up by inning five

Just as our thoughts of joining the Great Man sequence
lost out to a rakish dignity
in which we refused the groovy privilege
of the first-class airport lounge:
solar topees and free bocce balls
to lob across the rooftop topiary,
asserting themselves in the muffled *phuk*
of silver hitting sand.

Me, a hostile leftover
and you, a Paleolithic mother god—
hippy, odiferous and grinning
among the better thrift shop *bric-a-brac*.

#36

O.K.—it's Easter Sunday
I'm snug inside a gender
   & down to my salad weight

birdsong from the pollard trees
   leaves one feeling poleaxed,
fit to slim the moment
down to what it's good for:
     a community swim
       to the future
conceived as a succession of eternal instants
unflexing in hostile melodic situations
     improvised by martins
         in their androgyne symmetry

these are tough minutes
     between twilight and sunset
the satisfaction of one luminous regime
enjambed in the despotism of the next

the sound of beertrucks comes around
whispering thoughts of distributorships

light, a constant mothersource
flows through the panes
naughty cherubs installed
   to break over beautiful things

the flavor of persimmons in their context

eglantine, that useless blue
expedient Technicolor syllabaries

spell out the Inuit for
   "idiot"
      for "I"
for just plain dumb

a door closes—
    some of its promise
leaks off into air

to swell its tent in the actual,
        that spacious pitch
lodged somewhere between the
        kasbah
            and the souk. Minutes pile up
like monuments,
                phenomena that won't

stop happening—'x' instantiated in a weather
        that rains on our stellar prognostications
of a future
        with a literature
            for us

            The more I struggle,
                The tighter the noose
                    (Anthony Braxton)

if you feel real loose, like a long-necked goose
    the point is not to convince you it's a finger,
but to demonstrate its relation, albeit distant,
        to some larger structure

like freaks find one another
    by an inexorable logic,
two scooters that start on the very first pull
        converting *oohs* to ohms

paroxysms of saxophones
            arranged for maximum noise
imperial, as usual—

I pity the fool exogamous enough
to organize a panel
        around some of these issues:
to strum a self-pitying fado
where syrup is more *de rigueur*

including our oeuvre in a repertoire
    marked by a spectacular absence
of public gestures
        amidst the exacting rigors
        of successful cocktail banter

                (not that I buy the New Yorker)

Beautiful systems grind above us.
It's Easter; I'm down to my salad weight
the martins converge on new forms of despotism
coloring the seconds
    like a Loony Tunes cartoon,
some lippy and unrepentant,
others pissed off and massing in the hills.

#37

In this one she's on camera, building a daft chateau
of sugar cubes. And you, who blew a fortune
prizing almonds off the roof
caught sticking them back on with saccharine glee.

You're lashed to an aqueous jukebox.
The ladies inside cry: "Moby! Moby Dick!"
Lights fizz in their circuits
with nowhere much to go.
I wonder if inside it's comfortable

If they play my favorite pop songs,
if Meg, her trusty assistant, still broadcasts
counterfactual sexual advice.

Large groups of people have been found within these rooms
after the simulcast, naked, without their recipies.
Consensual hi-jinks with licorice sticks
and then the butch tanks—
Israel nibbling up Nablus, Palestine a lemon chiffon.
Captains, return to your persons.
Rememberers, sin by excess.

Sprinkle the cavern with pomegranate seeds
then buy the CD of me playing shofar—
shofar, father of saxophones.
Imagine them provoking us to air raids
then asking we rebuild their shitty walls.

Pelt the bride with acorns,
a local sign of prosperity.
A charming story explaining the presence of the plinth
has unfortunately just completely slipped my mind.

Cover the tabernacle with artful wings
but take care not to tell the seraphim.
On slow days they make hummus,
swap shopworn euhemerisms about Osiris.
The womenfolk chew it to an intoxicating pulp
then spit out the juice in this giant calabash.
These entertaining objects
were thought to be for gambling
but now it's been proposed they're little gods.

Remove your shoes before circumambulating
the dome. Pass thusly three times
through the purifying fire
in these special flame-retardant clothes.
The sexy figures in the upper frieze
should not be understood as erotic,
but as a touching plea for fertility.

Tonight's ceremony will require your bride's
virginity. Spread nard over the bedclothes
and charge it up to the hotel. The poppies mean
we're leaving. It was a once-in-a-lifetime
sort of thing—the seeds were used for visions
and the husks served as clothes.
On the airport concourse you'll notice a series
of fluorescent yellow cannisters: please put them down
at once. The people were so sorry when
we told them you were leaving—
that's why I think they're dancing
that funny little dance.

How to find safe passage
between the Scylla of garnished wages
and the Charybdis of subpar dental care?
How negotiate the *mare incognita* of preconscious verbal data
without pissing off the *vagina dentata* its excretions
will have to pass through? Into the exacting protocols
of the titty bar, how deeply should one probe?
The art of pleasing men is various—
if the bush insists on burning,
who am I to cast aside my dancing shoes?

Is pride a thing as intricate
as a tick's anatomy? Or is it a matter
of sucking down lemons
to the proper concentrate of lemonade?
Why insist on absconding with the spelling bee cash
if it ends only in the purchase
of a souped-up private language of one's own?
Ego is an autopsy
at which you're a guest but also its theater,
a space in which no detail is too small to be applauded, but only once
the scalpels go to town.

How to exit the graduation
without setting off the fire alarm?
Continue these pirate broadcasts
from the fell basement of world trade?
New breakthroughs are always on the verge of happening;
in the meantime, you are an accomplished
and sensual fire, in which the forms of the future
are visible almost continuously.

Shut the fuck up, Grasshopper—
the stones are trying to sing.
From the upper-story windows of the subdivision
Dawn exudes its rosiness,
windshields accumulate the moonlight
in little souvenirs of dew
and from my excellent vantage on the cineplex balustrade
I can see the arrondissement's most taxing problems:

Bad credit at Casa de Escrow;
spiritual longings from the hours of angry yoga
to the vapid late-morning commute;
Neofascist A-bombs slouching toward KinderCare.

Refuseniks of the senses! Provocateurs
against the color blue! In my poetics of personal
                              empowerment
Jesus affixes a question mark
to your already-golden brows;
the crowd thins, the doves disperse
but underneath the firetrucks
goldenrods smolder and bloom.

Congressmen of Acceptances! Revolutionaries
of the science of other people!
The future will forgive us
only our diminishment. The real moments of gentleness between
Friday's abrupt disappearance
and Monday's immense revenge
are surrounded by advanced possibilities for inaction.
Not one of us in these intervals
has grown less beautiful.
SHHHH! A choir of sexy Esquimaux
cries 'mush' from my wife's boudoir.
We were young, trés cool, and very much in love—
and then there's the matter of the ocelot.

#41

Chief Weemaway at summer camp
now introducing single scouts
at slinky postgraduate mixers,
dependent on pundits to run a wobbly Raj
whose frontiers shimmer at tiffin
through the jungle's insufferable wheeze.

We were moving into the lower echelons
of something not that important—
an honorable competence,
a cheap & seedy victory
in Victoria's teensier wars.
You, the fauna seemed to say, are that:
prime integer in a series
already complete with your absence;
a felicific calculus
assigning the ever-ambiguous
role of 'x' to you; a dervish spinning ciphers
in advance of the Queen's fusillade.

To what extent do the children repeat
the colonial airs of their parents?
Beating the Gurkhas to senseless shreds,
then having the carpets sent home?
Wave to the crowd of small and happy peoples—
a gathering with which to 'cope' or 'deal'.
Tomorrow the concrete will finally be accomplished
by its thieving double, fear.

#42

Speak of it one time in Portugal, and then
only in superlatives. If forced to ingest the pill
against your will, activate this tiny
radio-controlled device
and notify the Consulate at once.

Our man in Oporto
warns of a disreputable cabal
accumulating in the cafes—
familiarize yourself with the moodier lines
of Fernando Pessoa, from which their passwords are drawn.

Where the Tagus meets the docklands:
be most afraid of that. Memorize, then eat
this critical document. The river flows on
in its babble, the stalls in the market are lonely old roués
who whimper up to midnight feelingly. Prepare to liaise
with your contact here, Joaquim. The bars are getting
                                            empty.
Our safety, absurdly, has come to depend upon you.

As in the works of Cindy Sherman,
　　dirty bombs blow up the shopping malls.

The canvasses of Warhol project a cool surface
　　which may be the last retreat of the extrovert.

Motherwell, oddly, was awful to his mother
　　while Cornell wanted to see all New York disappear
in a bright ball of searing white flame.

Since the highly-publicized monkeyshines of the second-
　　generation New York School,
gossip embraces its urge to be theory.

Joseph Beuys reminds us
　　of the shamanistic impulse
at the root of all great art

While work from the most recent Biennale
　　calls into question the church-like position
of our urban American parking lots.

However controversial, Christo and his partner, Jean-Claude
　　invite us to think about how controversy itself
continues to fire tensions in the Middle East.

Like in the recent collages of Richard Hamilton,
　　in which the global thermometer
drops by a few degrees

Or the riotously-crowded canvasses
　　of Robert Rauschenberg,
which speak eloquently to the concerns of bigoted
　　　　　　　　　　　　　　　　Protestants

German neo-realist Gerhard Richter
　　grapples in trenchant, exhilarating ways
with issues of immigration and urban sprawl.

Sophie's Pick: Ape House, by Praxiteles.
I like how the picture tips its hat to something
classical, and how the green bursts from the canvas till
  my eyes, they want to bleed.

Visigoth Kotex.
Aramaen E-Z Off.
Mesopotamian Speed Dialing.

Mycenaean Bingo Night.
Etruscan Live/Work lofts.
P-Celt Listerine.

Avar Avon.
Thracian Dental Tape.
Deutero-Malay Meatless Entrees.

Choctaw Quik-Mart.
Arapahoe Pool Supply.
Potawottamie Wok Emporium.

Hittite Toothpaste.
Coptic Super Wash.
Paphlagonian Wrinkle Cream.

Aryan Rent-A-Van.
Samaritan Garden and Home.
Indo-European Shoe Repair.

Etrurian Cooling and Heating.
Frankish turkey franks.
Shang's: A Brasserie.

Phrygian Drive-In.
Nabataen Auto Parts.
Mezo-American Pets, Etc.

Merovingian Hair Club.
Nubian Body and Glass.
Achaemenid Shaving Cream.

Minoan Drain Solutions.
Palmyrene Carpet Showroom.
Proto-Ugaritic Limousines.

Assyrian Videoconferencing.
Punic Beauty Specialists.
Zoroastrian Coin-Op Superette.

Ozymandias Funeral Services.
Aztec Trash Removal.
Bulgar Beer.

Free Space:
Call Hominid Billboards.
Your Name Here.

First I began an agonizing trip to China,
then I was drawn by the opaline waters
of Venice, and finally of Rome. Personal voices
on cultural matters drew me away to
the drawing room, where Papa discoursed about Doges
And mother wrote Kansas for rent.

                It was a silly villa, really
but we were only being Spartan,
in terror of the fisherboys
retracing their parade to the Embassy.
Each year the outgoing Mayor
betrothed himself to the Adriatic, accompanied by unseemly weeping
and the tossing of an expensive ring
into the canal's ungrateful bowels. I saw
something wink from the casement
as a velveteen poltroon exercised his views

On Caravaggio. Later, at the séance
I felt the same gleam of recognition
clasping hands with the Countess, afraid to let go
in the Rosicrucian gloom.
As the table began to wobble
and ghostlight appeared in the mirror
Papa burst in, an anthology of gestures,
to shoo us outside for the equinox.

              Naked, abob in the Tiber
the Countess presents her sleek flanks
to Neptune, fisherboys and ghostly Doge
who abuse us with moonlight
monotonously. I dive for the brightness,
pull up anemones, slicken the river with a skin
of pomade. It slides in the moonlight, a China, a ring.
What sound does water make in Singapore?
Cities of vast opportunity await us,
Squirming with probabilities.

To execute a prim falcade
and strictly exclude nicknames from the eunuch's
vindictive ears—*that* would be just super
for the cenotaph. Mars waxing altruistic
unseats the nasty Shang. Each chariot
demands its Fisher King—a costly program, which,
sad for the annals of falconry, places these crazy sea-
                                       dragons
on the rarest of white jade pestles,
etched with poetic inscriptions
involving a deft comparison
between white snow falling on white blossoms

And the brutality of inscription
on a pestle of rare white jade.
When the first explorers saw this lush, green land
they wanted to keep it all for themselves
so named it TurnBackNowLand. Not only were the hawks
                                       not fooled
but after that, in TurnBackian lore,
Heron and Hawk were regarded not as enemies
but sisters, and today still hang together
above these desolate, overdeveloped hills.

Sit, Stella, and fondle my Afro
under midnight's urgent weather.
Maids of house and techno
  fancydance in vitro

      the stars, flaneurs
      of night's inverted city
       consider our position
       with the inwardness of cineastes

splayed nasturtiums:
    unfinished poems

 pigeons snapping upwards:
       whispers through broken fingers

not much elemental—
process riffles stillness
weird ivory ocean scudding
  wind voluting water

       the jewel is in the logo
         the jew
       is in the Logos

not much but stillness
lived it its thisness:
  this poem, this abundance

      stars in Ocean City
      wind voluting water

Come, Stella, and fondle my Afro
the jewel is in the logo
    nasturtiums
cling to poems, light
    splays in the water

     night,
it whispers downward: it sings
    and splays and sings.

Is not life more than food
and <u>basar</u> more than *malbush*?
un mystere d'amour dans le metal
                              repose.

The tankers are heavy
with frilly things—
pukka memsah'b pizza face
make eyes at station babu.

Select an extravagant menswear
for your meeting with Global Compliance.
Alight, Brian, from your grooved caracole
to applause of supper clubs.
If the middle class is sinking

Into luxury sedans, if the fellahin accede
to our generous dental plan,
if smoke from grandpa's meerschaum
should stain the Contessa's memoir,

who hands Ondine her dance card
without mixing up khedives?
To meet in the shady secrecy
of concrete parking structures, such

will be our business—to run
the little India of ourselves
with a languorous bureaucracy.

How lovely to shout up to your yacht tonight,
how nice to lash the rhododendrons
into tidy threnodies of red. How surreal
to be included in the after-hours jam,
enthusing "Man, it *swings* in here!"
       "Who's flatulent?"
         "Got Rilke?"

I have delicate lorgnettes in my back pocket,
but soon I'll be glissading
beneath June's gibbous moon.
Earthy dubs from a distant room
electrify the silent things,
making little scratches in the hip-hop
of other people's business. *Antigo*

e disante, old and distant, you and me
tethered in this restful Pleistocene, the stars bulged
like oranges in a humid orangery, nucleids unspooling
in their inevitable pavanes. How great to be present
at your underused vacation home,
how pleasant to commandeer the nightcaps
under midnight's urgent whine.
Yesterday I painted my icon of everything

On the breadbox atop the refrigerator—
tomorrow it will be exhibited in the lobby
of one of your downtown hotels.
How thoughtful that you planned the expedition
in just that way, and knew without asking
we'd like it: to make peace with a freeway
that only distantly honked for us,
to sleep in the cool Adirondacks
of somebody else's remembrance.

#50

Summer acrostic hotshot,
Urgent as a somnambulist.
Create in me a clean heart, Zardoz—
Krazy-glue gentile moils upon me.

Orangutans, start your gonads:
Not one of you gets out of Zaire alive.

The thing I learned at scribe camp:
Hermes is vowels. Graminivores
In igloos eat more teeth.
So much for that Hummer the

Orotund senator sent round—
She got spotted on the parkway, imploring
Apaches to land.
"My, what cheesy palms you have, Sir Swithin."
All I ever wanted was free beer.

Acknowledgements

These poems, identified by the first line, first appeared, often with entirely different titles, in the following publications:

Can We Have Our Ball Back? "Impurity's the watchword here," "A half-life in ingenious drag," "Memo to Britney," "You, a pub quiz Alexander."

Combo: "Mammogram the bildungsroman," "Sore and recusant in Memorex," "Erik the Red on Kickapoo Juice," " Consider the lilies," Legions of lesions on Janet's hale liver."

Mirage#4/Period(ical): "Caravansaries cavorting," "Some weeks later out of Tours," "You feel almost bad for the Babylon whores," "Richer than maple."

Moria: "Up what streets are your dependents wandering?"

The Muse Apprentice Guild: "Arguably a cicada," "The harlots of midnight," "In this one she's on camera," "Sprinkle the cavern," "To execute a prim falcade."

The San Francisco Reader: "To take this body back to its first ocean."

The San Jose Manual of Style: "The gates of horn," "Electric in the rest home."

Shampoo: "Seaplanes crashing through windowpanes," "Here at the garden's hot marges."

VeRT: "Sweethearts of what rodeo?," "I have seen Grandma's secretions," "Gulls hit the breeze," "O.K., it's Easter Sunday."